M000119795

DELANEY
STREET
PRESS

The Fisherman's
Book of Wisdom

The Fisherman's Book of Wisdom

A Treasury of Inspirational Quotations About the Joys of Fishing

by Criswell Freeman

©2000 by Delaney Street Press

All rights reserved. Except for brief quotes used in reviews, articles, or other media, no part of this book may be reproduced or transmitted in any form or by any means, electronic or mechanical, including photocopying, recording, or by information storage or retrieval system, without permission by the publisher.

DELANEY STREET PRESS
Nashville, TN: (800) 256-8584

ISBN 1-58334-070-X

The ideas expressed in this book are not, in all cases, exact quotations, as some have been edited for clarity and brevity. In all cases, the author has attempted to maintain the speaker's original intent. In some cases, material for this book was obtained from secondary sources, primarily print media. While every effort was made to ensure the accuracy of these sources, the accuracy cannot be guaranteed. For additions, deletions, corrections or clarifications in future editions of this text, please write DELANEY STREET PRESS.

Printed in the United States of America
Cover Design by Bart Dawson
Typesetting & Page Layout by Sue Gerdes

1 2 3 4 5 6 7 8 9 10 • 00 01 02 03 04 05 06

ACKNOWLEDGMENTS

The author gratefully acknowledges the helpful support of Angela Beasley Freeman, Dick and Mary Freeman, Mary Susan Freeman, Jim Gallery, and the entire team of professionals at DELANEY STREET PRESS and WALNUT GROVE PRESS.

For Bill Freeman

Table of Contents

Table of Contents

Introduction

Former President Jimmy Carter spoke for anglers everywhere when he observed, "After all these years, I still feel like a boy when I'm on a stream or lake." Such is the lure of fishing: It draws us in, takes us back in time, and connects us with a power much greater than our own.

If the big fish are biting —or even if they're not — devoted anglers need no prodding: As surely as the night follows day, so must fishermen follow their prey. Even in the face of overwhelming odds, ardent anglers find ways to wet a line, whether on blue waters, rivers, lakes, or backyard ponds. It is the nature of fishermen that they continually return to the water with new lures in their tackle boxes and fresh hope in their hearts.

This book celebrates the pleasures, the joys, and the lifetime lessons that are as much a part of fishing as rods and reels. So whether you fish for marlin or carp, trout or bass, salmon or catfish, take the quotations in this book to heart. And give thanks that you're a fisherman: Like President Carter, you'll remain forever young.

1

The Joy of Fishing

Izaak Walton observed, "No life is so happy and so pleasant as the life of the well-govern'd angler." Fishermen everywhere agree. The opportunity to go down to the water and catch fish is, for the avid angler, a heavenly pursuit.

The following pages describe the joys of fishing. May devoted anglers read these words and relive the simple pleasures of finding — and landing — the big one.

No fisherman ever fishes as much
as he wants to.

Geoffrey Norman

The two best times to go fishing are
when it's raining and when it's not.

Fisherman's Saying

Angling is the way to round out
a happy life.

Charles K. Fox

Angling is not only
a most agreeable
and delightful
amusement, it also
imparts health and
long life.

Palmer Hackle, Esq.

If you wish to be
happy for eight days,
kill your pig and eat it.
If you wish to be happy
for a lifetime,
learn to fish.

Chinese Proverb

For the true angler, fishing produces
a deep, unspoken joy, born of longing for
that which is quiet and peaceful, and
fostered by an inbred love of nature.

Thaddeus Norris

Fishing seems to be the favorite form
of loafing.

Ed Howe

A bad day fishing
still beats a good day
working.

Fisherman's Saying

When is the best season of the year
to go a-fishing? When you feel like it
and can leave home and business.
                                    Charles Bradford

The greatest angling success, more
valuable and satisfying than any trophy,
is teaching a young person to fish.
                                    Jim Palmer

If fishing interferes with your business,
give up your business.
                                    Sparse Grey Hackle

The charm of fishing
is that it is the pursuit
of what is elusive but
attainable, a perpetual
series of occasions
for hope.

John Buchan

I now believe that fishing is far more important than the fish.

Arnold Glasgow

Why do people go fishing?
Some say they fish to get fish.
This is obviously false.
John W. Randolph

'Tis not all of fishing to fish.
Izaak Walton

One thing becomes clearer as one
gets older and one's fishing experience
increases: the paramount importance
of one's fishing companions.
John Ashley-Cooper

I have fished through
fishless days that
I remember happily
and without regret.

Roderick Haig-Brown

The gods do not
deduct from a man's
allotted span the hours
spent in fishing.

Babylonian Proverb

Fishing is the chance to wash one's soul
with pure air, with the rush of the brook,
or with the shimmer of the sun
on blue water.
Herbert Hoover

Of all the world's enjoyments,
That ever valued were;
There's none of our employments
With fishing can compare.
Thomas D'Urfey

Fish come and go, but it is the memory
of afternoons on the stream that endure.
E. Donnall Thomas

The trout do not rise in the cemetery, so you better do your fishing while you are still able.

Sparse Grey Hackle

2

Finding the Fish

In order to catch a fish, one must first find it. Unfortunately, the fish's job, first and foremost, is to avoid detection, so the fisherman finds himself locked in a timeless game of hide-and-seek with his prey. The quotations in this chapter chronicle that unending war of wits versus instinct: the battle between fisherman and fish.

Time and territory are the two key
factors. Most people miss the biggest
fish in the lake because they're fishing
at the wrong spot at the wrong time.
Will Kirkpatrick

Most of the world is covered
with water. A fisherman's job is simple:
Pick out the right parts.
Charles F. Waterman

The wary angler in the
winding brook knows
the fish and where
to bait his hook.

Ovid

The best fisherman
in the world can't
catch them if they
aren't there.

Anthony Acerrano

When there are no
fish in one spot,
cast your hook
in another.

Chinese Proverb

The secret of successful angling
depends on learning the kind of water
the fish prefer, and then
concentrating on it.
Ted Trueblood

Four-fifths of the earth's surface is
covered with water, but only
five percent of that water
is good fishing.
Ted Trueblood

If you want to catch fish, you'd better
be fishing in the right pond.
Fisherman's Saying

The hardest part of fishing is learning
to read water.
Geoffrey Norman

You can't learn any stream by heart
in less than three seasons.
Arnold Gingrich

The years teach much which the days
never know.
Ralph Waldo Emerson

The first principle of reading water is this: Fish are found at the edges of things.

Charles F. Waterman

Every fishing water has its secrets....
To yield up these mysteries, it must be
fished with more than hooks.
Zane Grey

Nothing is ever simple about fish,
whether it's catching them
or understanding them.
A. J. McClane

A fishing notebook is invaluable,
and all serious anglers
should keep one.
Ted Trueblood

Learn to visualize the lake
        without the water.
                                    Jim Chapralis

Anybody can see the weeds.
        It takes a little practice to notice
        the less obvious features.
                                    Charles F. Waterman

Successful hunters and fishermen
        are precise observers of the world
        around them. They have to be
        in order to be successful.
                                    George Reiger

To be a good angler, one must have a
good knowledge of fish, for
to understand the quarry
is to defeat him.

Tiny Bennett

Learning to catch fish is not
difficult, but becoming reasonably
expert at it does require
time and study.

A. J. McClane

Angling may be said to be
like mathematics in that it can
never fully be learnt.

Izaak Walton

Ten percent of the
water holds ninety
percent of
the fish.

Dave Hughes

Ten percent of the
fishermen catch
ninety percent
of the fish.

Fisherman's Saying

When you are lucky
enough to find fish,
stay put.

Roger Bacon

3

Patient Fishing

When the fish decide not to bite, there's no use trying to convince them otherwise. All fish operate according to their own timetables, ignoring the impatient pleas of emotional anglers. Wise fishermen learn patience in the face of an empty net.

The following words of wisdom remind us what veteran anglers already know: When the fish aren't biting, a pleasant disposition is the most valuable tool in the tackle box.

Whether you fish tournaments or just
enjoy the occasional weekend trip,
patience is a virtue when
it comes to fishing.

Roger Bacon

The greatest fishing secret ever?
Patience.

Donald Jack Anderson

You have to be prepared to sit all day
long and wait for that big one to bite.

Bob Crupi

Be patient and calm —
for no one can catch
fish in anger.

Herbert Hoover

There is a final
moment of unyielding
patience which,
in angling, so often
makes the difference
between fish and
no fish.

Sparse Grey Hackle

You can't catch fish on a dry line.
Fisherman's Saying

If you want fish, fish.
German Proverb

Adopt the pace of nature;
her secret is patience.
Ralph Waldo Emerson

So frequent the casts.
        So seldom the strikes.
                                Arnold Gingrich

In order to be a successful angler,
 you must first accept one simple fact:
There are times when fishing is tough.
                                Roger Bacon

Be content: The sea hath fish enough.
                                Thomas Fuller

There is a rhythm to an angler's life
and a rhythm to his year.
Nick Lyons

A thousand fishing trips go by,
indistinguishable from one another,
and then suddenly one comes along
that is fatefully perfect.
A. J. McClane

You really have to be ready at all times.
Big fish hit when you least expect it.
Bill Murphy

A good angler must bring a large
measure of hope and patience.
Izaak Walton

The hasty angler loses the fish.
Fisherman's Saying

A fisherman has many dreams.
Some dreams, even those of a
fisherman, come true.
Zane Grey

The best fish swim deep.

Thomas Fuller

There's no taking fish in dry breeches.

Cervantes

If you want to catch more fish,
use more hooks.

George Allen

All you need to be a fisherman is patience and a worm.

Herb Shriver

Persistence, for the fisherman, is a virtue that transcends patience.

A. J. McClane

Luck affects everything;
let your hook always be
cast. In the stream where
you least expect it,
there will be fish.

Ovid

4

Fish Tales

An old Japanese saying reminds us, "A fish is larger for being lost." This bit of wisdom from the Orient acknowledges the well-documented fact that anglers tend to exaggerate. A lot.

The following quotations celebrate the fisherman's propensity for hyperbole. Thoughtful readers are wise to remember that in the world of angling, the biggest part of any fish is usually its tale.

Anglers have a way of romanticizing their battles with fish.

Ernest Hemingway

The biggest fish I ever caught was the one that got away.

Willard Spencer

So long as imagination tempts and
hope persists, there will remain that
undiscovered star of the angler's
firmament, that biggest fish of all,
the one that got away.
Frederick White

Bragging may not bring happiness,
but no man having caught a large fish
goes home through the alley.
Anonymous

It is not a fish until it is on the bank.
Irish Proverb

A fish on the hook is better than ten
in the brook.
Fisherman's Saying

Nothing grows faster
than a fish from the
time he bites until the
time he gets away.

Fisherman's Saying

5

The Right Kind of Tackle

The right kind of tackle can make the difference between a king-sized catch and an empty net. Perhaps that's why fisherman are *so* particular about their equipment. And perhaps that also explains why acquisitive anglers spend the winter months thumbing through catalogues in search of new fishing gear. In this chapter, we explore the correlation between a well-stocked tackle box and a well-filled cooler full of fish.

The joys of fishing are not confined to the hours near the water.

Herbert Hoover

Prepare your tackle. When you hook a big fish, it is impossible to retie a knot or change a leader.

Jim Chapralis

Unless you have a ritual for getting your tackle box ready, no one will regard you as a serious fisherman.

John W. Randolph

A good fisherman can
secure many regenerative
hours in winter,
polishing up the
rods and reels.

Herbert Hoover

A fisherman will spend
almost as much time
in the tackle shops
as he will upon
a trout stream.

William Hjortsberg

Fishing equipment is fun.

Roderick Haig-Brown

One of the turning points of my life
was when I got my first
bait-casting outfit.

Jimmy Carter

An old tackle box can be a gold mine
of long-forgotten treasures and a place
to find old fishing memories.

Jim Porter

A good rod is without doubt
the angler's chief requisite.
Hardy Brothers Catalogue, 1886

Does a custom rod catch more fish?
I answer with a qualified
but excited "Yes!"
Ian Scott

Your outfit may be elaborate, or
it may be a cane pole. Fortunately, the
size of your kit is no indication of the
pleasure you derive.
Jack Randolph

Fishing is not necessarily expensive…
though it can be.

Joe Panfalone

A dirty-looking lure marred by a year's
worth of abuse or neglect won't produce
nearly as well as a squeaky clean one
with hooks honed to
a piercing edge.

Tommy Martin

Taking care of your fishing line is an
extremely important part of maintaining
your tackle. Change lines often.

Sam Anderson

Venture a small fish to catch a great one.
Thomas Fuller

You can catch your next fish with a piece
of the last.
Oliver Wendell Holmes

He that would catch fish
must first venture his bait.
Ben Franklin

The reason life
sometimes seems dull
is because we do not
perceive the importance
and excitement
of getting bait.

Henry Van Dyke

Give a man a fish and
you feed him for a day.
Teach a man to fish
and you feed him
for a lifetime.

Ancient Proverb

6

The Great Outdoors

Roderick Haig-Brown spoke for all anglers when he confessed, "Perhaps fishing is, for me, only an excuse to be near rivers." Haig-Brown understood that the greatest attraction for the fisherman is often the setting in which the fishing takes place.

The outdoorsman who goes down to the water in search of fish is advised to pause and take ample time to appreciate the scenery. The sport of fishing is played out in God's arena; the opportunity to lose oneself in the quiet beauty of nature is surely one of the sport's greatest appeals.

Nature is always hinting at us.

Robert Frost

God is making the world, and the show
is so grand and beautiful and exciting
that I have never been able to study
any other.

John Muir

Nature is the art of God.

Dante

We can never have enough of Nature.

Henry David Thoreau

One of the great
charms of angling
is that of all the sports,
it affords the best
opportunity to enjoy
the wonders and beauty
of nature.

J. J. Manley

Fishing is more than fish;
  it is the vitalizing lure to outdoor life.
Herbert Hoover

Once in a while, spend a week
  in the woods. Wash your spirit clean.
John Muir

I have never been happier, more
  exhilarated, at peace, inspired, and aware
    of the grandeur of the universe and
  greatness of God than when I find myself
  in a natural setting not much changed
      from the way He made it.
Jimmy Carter

If I fished only to capture fish, my fishing
trips would have ended long ago.
Zane Grey

The angler forgets most of the fish he
catches, but he does not forget the streams
and lakes in which they were caught.
Charles K. Fox

As the angler looks back, he thinks less
of individual captures and days
than of scenes in which he fished.
Lord Grey of Fallondon

Wherever the trout are, it's beautiful.

Thomas Masaryck

All our Concord waters have two colors at least: one when viewed at a distance, and another, more proper, close at hand.
Henry David Thoreau

Every country boy is entitled to a creek.
Havilah Babcock

A crick is a distinctly separate entity from a creek....After all, a creek is merely a creek, but a crick is a crick.
Patrick McManus

Fishing isn't always about fishing.
Greg Milner

Fishing is more than fish. Fishing is the great occasion when we may return to the fine simplicity of our forefathers.
Herbert Hoover

Many of the most highly publicized events of my presidency are not nearly as memorable or significant in my life as fishing with my daddy.
Jimmy Carter

Let children walk with nature.

John Muir

Fishing is timeless and ageless, and it's a family tradition that should be passed on to future generations.

Virginia Pierce

A man never stands so tall as when he stoops to help a child fish.

Jim Porter

If you instill in your child a love of the
outdoors and an appreciation of nature,
you will have given him a treasure
no one can take away.

Ted Trueblood

Nature never did betray
The heart that loved her.

William Wordsworth

There is something in fishing that tends
to produce a gentleness of spirit
and a pure sincerity of mind.

Washington Irving

We need the tonic
of the wilderness.

Henry David Thoreau

7

A Day Spent Fishing

Fishing, when done properly, is a pure, joyous experience. The wise angler never allows frustration or anger to invade the quiet sanctity of the fishing trip. Instead, he savors his time on the water, whether the fish are biting or not.

It has been said that a bad day fishing beats a good day spent doing nearly anything else. But seasoned anglers understand that there are really no such things as "bad" fishing days. There are only days when overanxious fishermen don't fully recognize all the good things that surround them.

Every intelligent sportsman knows
that the greatest rewards of hunting
and fishing are irresistible.
Ted Trueblood

I have experienced such simple joy
in the trivial matters of fishing and
sport as might formerly inspire
the muse of Homer
or Shakespeare.
Henry David Thoreau

The angler is never a has-been. He
enjoys a lifetime of participation which
continues through noon, then on into the
sunset, and even into the eventide of life.
Charles K. Fox

Love of nature is a common language
that can transcend political and social
boundaries.
Jimmy Carter

Nature is an unlimited broadcasting
station through which God speaks to us
every hour — if we will only tune in.
George Washington Carver

I know of no optimism so great as that which perennially blooms in the heart of a fisherman.

Burton L. Spiller

Fishing greats, whether they realize it or not, practice PFA: Positive Fishing Approach.

Jim Chapralis

Fishermen are an optimistic class, or they would not be fishermen.

Herbert Hoover

All things come to those who bait.

Fisherman's Saying

A fisherman is
always hopeful —
nearly always more
hopeful than he has
any right to be.

Roderick Haig-Brown

There is always something wonderful about a new fishing adventure trip. Fishing is like Jason's quest for the Golden Fleece.

Zane Grey

We fishermen dream far more often
of our favorite sport than other men
dream of theirs.

Will H. Dilg

Even the thousandth trip to the same
old fished-out stream begins with
renewed hope, with unfailing faith.

Zane Grey

I have laid aside business
and gone a-fishing.

Izaak Walton

8

A Tackle Box Full of Fishing Tips

Savvy anglers have much to teach, and all fisherman, no matter how experienced, have much to learn. In this chapter we share an assortment of timely tips designed to help hook the one that might otherwise have gotten away.

All veteran anglers have their tricks
of the trade...usually you have to fish
a long time to pick them up.
Wheeler Johnson

Anglers are not born, they are made
by circumstances, and sometimes
it takes a long time to get the
right circumstances together.
John W. Randolph

Casting is not the end of knowledge.
In fact it is only the beginning.
Geoffrey Norman

Angling is an art worthy of the knowledge and practice of a wise man.

Izaak Walton

My best tip: find an expert to teach you how to fish.

Dirk Mewes

The fisherman who isn't plagued with suggestions is fishing alone.

Beatrice Cook

Man can learn
a lot from fishing.
When the fish are
biting, no problem in
the world is big
enough to be
remembered.

Oa Battista

The great charm of fly-fishing is that
we are always learning.
Theodore Gordon

Beyond every bend in a stream lies
a new fishing challenge, for no rapids or
pool is just like the previous one.
Dick Sternberg

Every lesson you learn, no matter
where you learn it, transfers to all other
rivers, no matter where you fish.
Dave Hughes

A man that goeth to the river for his pleasure must understand the Sun, and the Wind, the Moon, and the Stars, and set forth his tackle accordingly.

Thomas Barker

If you take your boat into the shallow waters, you had better know where the stumps are.

Fisherman's Saying

Some fishermen see no fish and
foolishly believe that the river is empty.
Henry Van Dyke

You've got to be ready to set the hook
when the fish strikes...otherwise,
you don't hook the fish.
Mark Hicks

You just never know when that next
big fish is going to show up.
Bill Murphy

Be especially attentive to noise
when fishing in shallow or clear water.
Keep voices low.

Ken Schultz

If you need a piece of equipment, make
it as light as possible. If you don't
need it, leave it at home.

Sparse Grey Hackle

One of the greatest dangers in fishing
is the danger of succumbing to the
temptation of all the gizmos, do-dads,
and whats-its available to the fisherman.

Joe Panfalone

Fisherman are advised to carry the following essentials: a water bottle, sunblock, snack food, and a raincoat.

Dirk Mewes

My advice is go often and visit many localities. Kill no more fish than you require for your own eating, and do that in the most scientific manner.

Charles Bradford

Consider building a rod for yourself.

Ian Scott

Catch no more fish than you can salt.
Fisherman's Saying

Throw the little ones back.
Fisherman's Saying

The fish is not so much your quarry
as your partner.
Arnold Gingrich

A good game fish is too valuable to be caught only once.

Lee Wulff

Fishing is more than a sport. It is a way of thinking and doing, a way of reviving the mind and body.

Roderick Haig-Brown

Fishing is not so much getting fish as it is a state of mind.

Herbert Hoover

By common consent, fishing is the most peaceful of all forms of sport.

H. T. Sheringham

9

Observations

We conclude with a few observations about the fishing life. Enjoy!

One of the charms of the sport is its infinite complexity. The wood has enough depth and richness to reward a lifetime of quiet, perspective searching.
Roderick Haig-Brown

To paraphrase a deceased patriot, I regret that I have only one life to give to my fly fishing.
Robert Traver

Older anglers know that misfortune is but a proper contrast to the good days astream.
A. J. McClane

No one is born an artist nor an angler.
Izaak Walton

If a man fishes hard, what is he going
to do easy?
Roy Blount, Jr.

Any man who pits his intelligence
against a fish and loses has it coming.
John Steinbeck

The skillful angler
must be full of
humble thoughts.

Gervase Markham

No matter how good a man gets
at fishing, he'll never land every fish
he hooks.

A. J. McClane

There was never an angler who lived
but that there was a fish capable of
taking the conceit out of him.

Zane Grey

Pride is surely the most unbecoming
of all vices in a fisherman.

Henry Van Dyke

Fishing is a constant
reminder of the
democracy of life, of
humility, and of human
frailty. The forces of
nature discriminate
for no man.

Herbert Hoover

Next to prayer, fishing is the most personal relationship of man.

Herbert Hoover

Many men go fishing
all of their lives without
knowing that it is not
fish they are after.

Henry David Thoreau

He who is content
to "not-catch" fish
will have his time and
attention free for the
accumulation of a
thousand experiences.

Sparse Grey Hackle

So many fish, so little time.
Fisherman's Saying

The contentment which fills the mind
of the angler at the close of the day's
sport is one of the chiefest
charms in his life.
Rev. William Cowper Prime

The music of angling is more
compelling to me than anything
contrived in the greatest
symphony hall.
A. J. McClane

The fisherman loves to row out in the
stillness of the mists of the morning when
the lake is like polished black glass.

Ernest Lyons

Surely one of the richest bounties of
angling is to grow deeply intimate with
the inner life of the world of nature,
and in doing so, to come closer
to your deepest self.

Nick Lyons

What do guides do on their days off? The best ones go fishing.

Dave Vedder

Fishing is more fun than baseball, watermelon and barbecues combined.

Mark Romanack

There is distinct similarity between cattle and casters in that each regards the grass as being greener on the other side of the fence.

Charles K. Fox

I knew an old fisherman who said he enjoyed the times when the fish weren't biting, for then he had time to see and hear all the things he would miss if he were too busy hauling in fish.

Archibald Rutledge

In the wilderness is the salvation
        of mankind.
Henry David Thoreau

True wisdom consists in not departing
from nature and in molding our conduct
      to her laws and models.
Seneca

Though we travel the world over to find
the beautiful, we must carry it with us
      or we find it not.
Ralph Waldo Emerson

It is not the fish we
catch that counts....
It is the joyous rush
of the brook, and the
contemplation of
the eternal rush
of the stream.

Herbert Hoover

The time must come to
all of us, who live long,
when memory is more
than prospect. An angler
who reaches this stage
and reviews the pleasures
of life will be glad
he was an angler.

Lord Grey of Fallondon

Fishing is the eternal
Fountain of Youth.

Herbert Hoover

Sources

About
DELANEY STREET PRESS

DELANEY STREET PRESS publishes books designed to inspire and entertain readers of all ages. DELANEY STREET books are distributed by WALNUT GROVE PRESS. For more information, call 1-800-256-8584.

About the Author

Criswell Freeman is a Doctor of Clinical Psychology living in Nashville, Tennessee. In addition to this text, Dr. Freeman is also the author of many other books including his bestselling self help book *When Life Throws You a Curveball, Hit It*.